Silly Joke Books

SILLY KNOCK-KNOCK JOKES

by Michael Dahl

PEBBLE
a capstone imprint

Published by Pebble, an imprint of Capstone
1710 Roe Crest Drive, North Mankato, Minnesota 56003
capstonepub.com

Library of Congress Cataloging-in-Publication Data is available on the Library of Congress website.
ISBN: 9781977131638 (hardcover)
ISBN: 9781977154880 (ebook PDF)

Summary: A collection of knock-knock jokes for young readers.

Editorial Credits
Editor: Christianne Jones; Designer: Brann Garvey and Mighty Media; Media Researcher: Jo Miller; Production Specialist: Laura Manthe

Image Credits
Shutterstock: Anna Kucherova, 14, vegetables, aquariagirl1970, 13, grill, asawinimages, 12, gecko, Bradley Blackburn, 10, kangaroo, Cheryl Casey, 20, pigtails, Chones, 14, keyhole, CobraCZ, 3, grey_and, 16, spoon, Grigoreva Alina, 5, Ian Dyball, Cover, eyes, innakreativ, 14, pecan, 15, pecan, insta_photos, 18, girl, irin-k, 9, bee, Iva Vagnerova, 4, javi_indy, 8, eye, kah loong lee, 11, khlungcenter, 16, spider, Krakenimages.com, 6, girl, 13, gorilla, Le Do, 14, butter, M Kunz, 10, cow, M. Unal Ozmen, 16, ice cream cone, marekuliasz, 19, canoe, paddle, naito29, 9, girl, NeydtStock, 20, clogs, Oleksandr Kostiuchenko, 8, keyhole, Paul Vowles, Cover, doors, Roman Samborskyi, 17, feet, Sandra Foyt, 21, Sorapop Udomsri, 15, girl, souloff, design element, stockcreations, 17, puppet, SunflowerMomma, 12, owl, Surasak Klinmontha, 24, SweetLemons, 14, eyes, 19, eyes, Syda Productions, 7, Tanya Sid, 6, walnuts, Vectorpocket, 18, ghost, Yevhenii Chulovskyi, 19, lake

Printed and bound in China. PO4205

Table of Contents

HELLO!

NUTTY NAMES

KNOCK!
KNOCK!

4

Knock, knock.
Who's there?

Harry.
Harry who?

Harry up and answer the door to find out!

Knock, knock.
Who's there?

Ben.
Ben who?

Ben waiting out here for 10 minutes!

Knock, knock.
Who's there?

Anita.
Anita who?

**Anita use the bathroom.
Let me in!**

Knock, knock.
Who's there?

Justin.
Justin who?

Justin time for dinner.

OVER THERE!

Knock, knock.
Who's there?

Cash.
Cash who?

No thanks. I prefer walnuts.

Knock, knock.
Who's there?

Olive.
Olive who?

Olive next door.

Knock, knock.
Who's there?

Amanda.
Amanda who?

**Amanda fix
your door!**

7

KNOCK! KNOCK!

Knock, knock.
Who's there?

Luke.
Luke who?

Luke through the keyhole and see for yourself!

Knock, knock.
Who's there?

Lena.
Lena who?

Lena little closer, and I'll tell you another joke.

8

Knock, knock.
Who's there?

Norma Lee.
Norma Lee who?

Normally I ring the doorbell, but it isn't working.

Knock, knock.
Who's there?

Abbey.
Abbey who?

Abbey stung me!

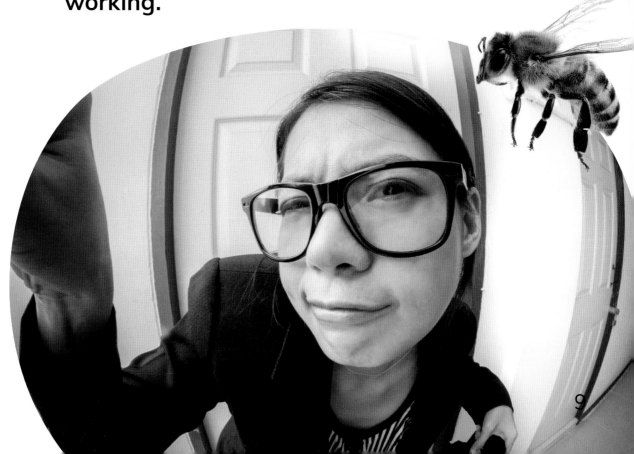

9

ANIMAL ANTICS

Knock, knock.
Who's there?

Kanga.
Kanga who?

No! It's a kangaroo.

Knock, knock.
Who's there?

Cows go.
Cows go who?

No, cows go moo!

MOO...

ACHOOO!

Knock, knock.
Who's there?

Hatch.
Hatch who?

Bless you!

Knock, knock.
Who's there?

Viper.
Viper who?

Viper nose, it's running!

11

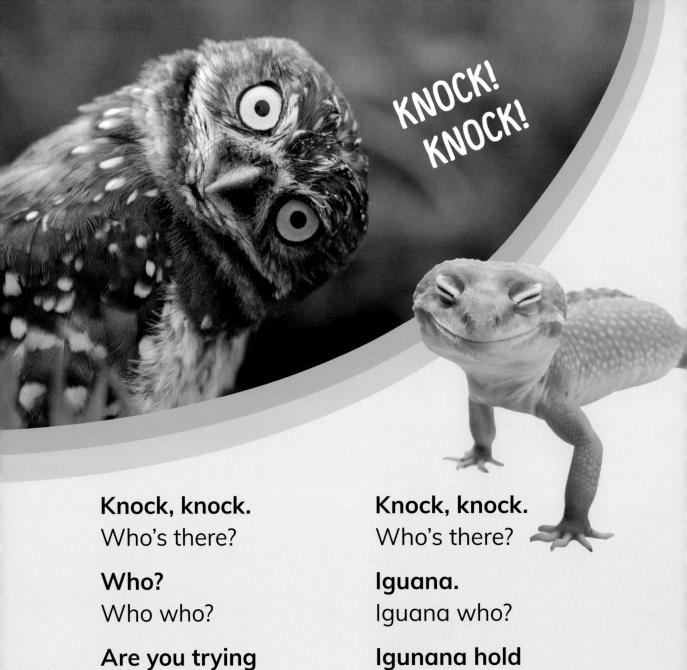

KNOCK!
KNOCK!

Knock, knock.
Who's there?

Who?
Who who?

**Are you trying
to be an owl?**

Knock, knock.
Who's there?

Iguana.
Iguana who?

**Igunana hold
your hand.**

12

Knock, knock.
Who's there?

Gorilla.
Gorilla who?

**Gorilla me a
burger please!**

NOM! NOM! NOM!

FOOD FUNNIES

Knock, knock.
Who's there?

Lettuce.
Lettuce who?

Lettuce in, please!

Knock, knock.
Who's there?

Beets.
Beets who?

Beets me! You're the one knocking.

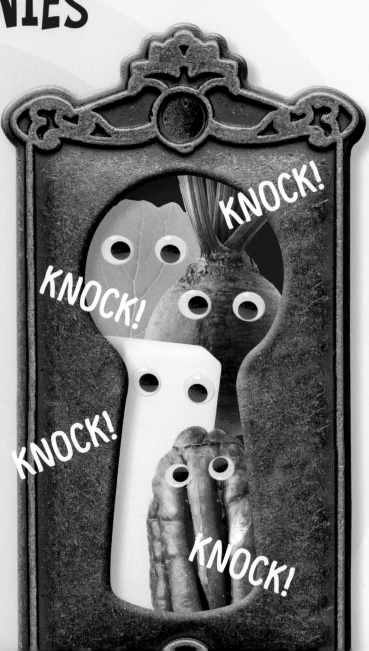

Knock, knock.
Who's there?

Butter.
Butter who?

**Butter bring an umbrella.
It's supposed to rain.**

Knock, knock.
Who's there?

Pecan.
Pecan who?

**Pecan someone
your own size.**

Knock, knock.
Who's there?

Water.
Water who?

Water you doing today?

Knock, knock.
Who's there?

Ice scream.
Ice scream who?

**Ice scream when
I see a spider.**

16

Knock, knock.
Who's there?

Pudding.
Pudding who?

Pudding on your shoes before your socks is a terrible idea.

KNOCK-KNOCK CRAZINESS

KNOCK!
KNOCK!

Knock, knock.
Who's there?

Boo.
Boo who?

You don't need to cry about it!

YOU'RE
WELCOME!

Knock, knock.
Who's there?

Tank.
Tank who?

You're welcome.

Knock, knock.
Who's there?

Canoe.
Canoe who?

**Canoe come out
and play?**

Knock, knock.
Who's there?

Spell.
Spell who?

W-H-O

Knock, knock.
Who's there?

Wooden shoe.
Wooden shoe who?

Wooden shoe like to know!

Knock, Knock.
Who's there?

Wah.
Wah who?

Why are you so excited?

Knock, knock.
Who's there?

Stopwatch.
Stopwatch who?

**Stopwatch you're doing,
and let me in!**

Knock, knock.
Who's there?

Little old lady.
Little old lady who?

**I didn't know you
could yodel!**

YODEL-
AY-EE-
OOOO

21

ACTIVITY: KNOCK-KNOCK DOOR HANGER

What you need:

- paper
- markers or crayons
- string
- tape
- scissors

What you do:

1. Cut a piece of paper into a rectangle shape. Make sure it's not too big to hang under your doorknob.

2. Write your favorite knock-knock joke on the paper.

3. Draw a picture or add fun designs to match the joke.

4. Cut a piece of string to add to your hanger. Measure it over your doorknob to make sure it fits.

5. Tape the string ends to the top part of your paper.

6. Any time someone wants to enter your room, make them knock and tell the joke.

GLOSSARY

canoe (kuh-NOO)—a small, shallow boat that people move through water with paddles

hatch (HACH)—to break out of an egg

nutty (NUHT-ee)—funny and silly

yodel (YOH-duhl)—to sing in a voice that changes rapidly between high and low sounds

READ MORE

Dahl, Michael. *Michael Dahl's BIG Book of Jokes.* North Mankato, MN: Capstone, 2020.

Pellowski, Michael J. *Mega-funny Jokes & Riddles.* New York: Sterling, 2017.

Riddle, H.A. *Laugh Yourself Silly Knock-Knock Jokes for Kids 2.* Tucson, AZ: Lonotek, 2018.

INTERNET SITES

Enchanted Learning
www.enchantedlearning.com/
jokes/topics/knockknock.shtml

Kidactivities
kidactivities.net/knock-knock-jokes

THE END

INDEX